America's Rural Yesterday

Volume III: At Home & In Town

© 2014 Mischka Press Publishing
Publisher of Rural Heritage Magazine

Publisher's Cataloging-in-Publication
(Provided by Quality Books, Inc.)

America's rural yesterday. Volume III, At home & in town /
 featuring the photography of J.C. Allen & Son ; edited
 by Joe Mischka.
   pages cm
   LCCN 2012953873
   ISBN 9781882199082

   1. Agriculture--United States--History--Pictorial
works. 2. Family farms--United States--History--
Pictorial works. 3. Country life--United States--
History--Pictorial works. 4. Cities and towns--United
States--History--Pictorial works.   I. Mischka, Joe,
editor. II. J. C. Allen & Son, photographer.
III. Title: At home & in town IV. Title: At home and in
town.

S520.A44 2014   630'.973
                          QBI14-600183

Contents

Introduction 4

1 Time in the Parlor...6

2 At the Family Table..22

3 In the Kitchen...30

4 Housework 44

5 Going to Town 56

6 In Town 72

7 Shopping...92

8 At School..106

9 Leisure Time..122

Introduction — A Simpler Time.

The small town near the farm where I grew up in the late 1960s was a lot like the towns pictured in the J.C. Allen photos in this book. The kitchens, dining rooms and parlors in the farmhouses featured here are a lot like the rooms in my house and like those in the homes of family, friends and neighbors I visited when I was young.

I know this is true for many of you looking at this book.

The coal or wood cookstove in the kitchen might have been a different model, but you remember the smells that came from it during the first fire of the morning before the flue was warmed and drawing well. You recall the sounds the hinged oven door made when it was opened, the clangs and clatters that came from the stovelids being lifted and lowered into place.

The radio you grew up listening to may have looked different from the ones in this book, but you remember how it crackled and popped as it was tuned from one station to the next. I remember how the radio my grandfather built himself from parts hummed when it was powered on.

Many of these photos will bring back fond memories of simpler, slower and more comfortable times. However, for the tired woman hand-wringing the laundry before hanging it on the line, or the man shoveling coal from the wagon to the wheelbarrow and to the coal chute, it was a harder time, too.

One of the things common to most of the J.C. Allen photos I have pored over is the look of contentment and satisfaction on the faces of the people in them. It was a time of hard work and long days but often spent in the company of friends, family and neighbors. Where today a farmer or factory worker can spend most of his or her time alone, operating the labor-saving machines, men and women of the early 20th Century often worked together, side by side.

This cultivated a sense of community and belonging that is absent from a lot of our lives today. Whenever we spend time at a church function, a school fundraiser, or a neigborhood block party, we get a morsel of this type of brotherhood.

Of course, life back then also meant dangerous isolation, particularly for neighbors living down remote dirt roads yet to be connected to a telephone party line.

I enjoy looking at these photos and remember my childhood and imagine what life was like when my parents were children before me. Rather than bemoan the loss of this way of life, I try to distill what makes that time so wonderful and seek out moments in places reminiscent of them. For when you remove the cell phones, video screens, rushing traffic and other frantic distractions in our lives, what remains are the people and animals in our lives and the places we together call home. Life today can more closely mimic life back then if we only make the effort.

— Joe Mischka

Rest time on the front porch of S.C. Malsbary, Romney, Indiana.

Above. Mr. & Mrs. Herman Heaton of Russiaville, Indiana, play a card game while their daughter looks on. 1938.

Upper Left. The Heaton family relax in their well-appointed parlor. Father reads the paper while mother does needlepoint and daughter tunes the radio. A lovely stove on the right keeps the scene cozy.

Left. An early evening scene with a multi-generational game of Bingo, likely in a house in town.

Opposite. The Joe Kerkhoff family of rural Lafayette, Indiana, listens to the radio in their farm home.

8   America's Rural Yesterday

The telephone party line brought many positive changes to rural life.

In addition to providing a source of news and gossip to combat the isolation, the phone also made it possible for neighbors to call and summon help in the event of a fire or other disaster.

Time in the Parlor

Each household on the party line had a specific "ring," a combination of short and long rings, to let everyone know who was getting a call. It was pretty well understood that if you got a call, most everyone else on the line was listening in.

The phone was typically placed near a staircase to be close to both levels of the house. In the photo above, the Tarvine family of rural Kentucky built a porthole into the staircase wall to make the phone even more accessible.

10 America's Rural Yesterday

Time in the Parlor

Opposite. Eight stockings hanging over the fireplace and eight children listen attentively as grandfather reads to them.

Above. Grandma reads to three kids while a portable gas lamp provides light. Notice the scissor holder behind the young girl's head.

Right. Mr. and Mrs. Fred Peavey read to their grandson. 1935.

Left. An organ accompanies this group of singers. 1931.

Opposite Top Left. The small dog seems to thoroughly enjoy the music made by the mother and two daughters.

Opposite Top Right. What appears to be a family band rehearses. The lettering on the bass drum is a little worn but may say "Lemings Musical Kids."

Opposite Bottom Left. The piano is pushed up against the door in this photo where a family sings together a Sunday hymn. 1934.

Opposite Bottom Right. Sister and brother play "Farewarell to Arms" on the piano and saxaphone while the rest of the family reads, dog included.

Time in the Parlor 13

14   America's Rural Yesterday

Time in the Parlor **15**

Opposite. Spending a winter afternoon making plans and looking through vegetable and flower seed catalogues. 1932.

Above Right. The note on the back of this photo says "Modern lighting in the farm home of Byron Legg near Windgall, Indiana.

Below Right. Reading by the light of a kerosene lamp.

16   America's Rural Yesterday

Opposite. The daughter cuts cloth into strips which the mother braids into a rug.

Below. A fire warms a woman knitting in a leather rocking chair and a cat intrigued by her ball of yarn.

Right. Ann Ostrander of West Lafayette, Indiana, embroiders in an upholstered chair.

18 America's Rural Yesterday

Left. A successful farmer kept accurate records.

Below. A farmer refers to his copy of "Farm Business Summary for Indiana's Type-of-Farming Area 5 Medium Farms," 1938.

Right. The radio helps this farmer keep track of commodity markets in 1936.

Time in the Parlor   19

20 America's Rural Yesterday

Above Left. Mr. and Mrs. Daniel Bechtol and their son, of Goshen, Indiana, with their farm radio in 1928.

Above. Wilbur Wilkey of Kengland, Indiana, reads while Mrs. Wilkey tunes in their farm radio.

Left. Father and son with their farm hats at their feet, reading and listening to the radio. 1929.

Opposite. The caption on the back of the photo reads "Mr. and Mrs. J.B. Douhit, Jr., of Pendleton, South Carolina, enjoy their modern farm home." 1927.

Time in the Parlor 21

22 America's Rural Yesterday

Left. Dinnertime at the farm home of Mr. and Mrs. Alpha Gilmore, operators of a dairy farm near Jeffersonville, Indiana.

Opposite. Extended family and other farm help were often included in the noontime meal, which also featured plenty of farm-raised food. 1938.

Chapter 2
At the Family Table

Above. Kitchen interior and electrical equipment in the farm home of Mr. and Mrs. W.Y. Hartsough of North Manchester, Indiana. 1932.

At The Family Table   **25**

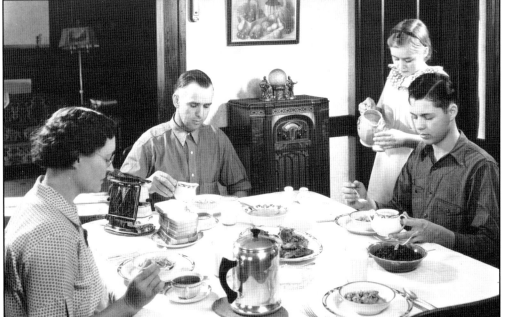

Above Left. Men washed their hands and combed their hair before sitting down for the noontime meal.

Above. A family gathers in the dining room on the farm of Mr. and Mrs. O.M. Herod, Mardsville, West Virginia.

Left. Breakfast in 1936.

26   America's Rural Yesterday

Above. Farmers were called in from the field by their wives or daughters ringing the dinner bell.

At The Family Table 27

Above Left. Sunday dinner at the T.R. Johnston family of West Lafayette, Indiana.

Above. Breakfast in 1933.

Left. Everyone is dressed in their Sunday finery at this family dinner.

28 America's Rural Yesterday

Above. A formal dinner in 1931.

At The Family Table   29

Above. The presentation of the holiday turkey at dinner in 1942.

30   America's Rural Yesterday

Above. Mrs. Daniel Bechtol of Goshen, Indiana, checks the roast in her Hotpoint electric range.
Opposite. The kitchen in the home of Mrs. Chas. O. Lee in West Lafayette, Indiana, in 1937.

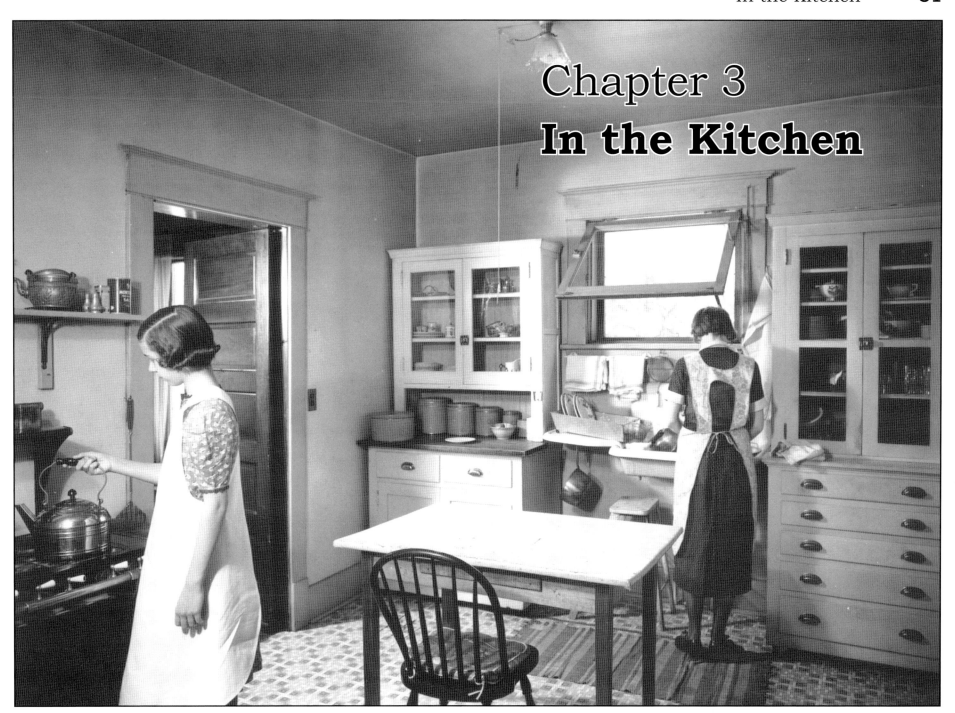

Chapter 3
In the Kitchen

Above and opposite. A variety of early ranges and cookstoves.

In the Kitchen

34 America's Rural Yesterday

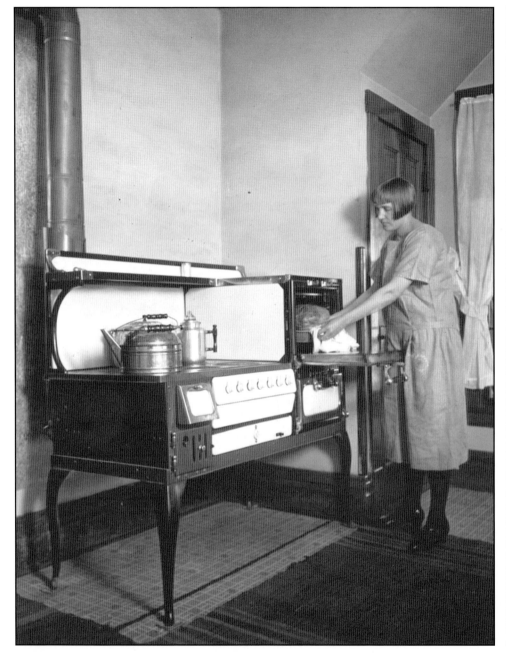 

Left. Mrs. R.H. Bainer and her combination coal and electric range. **Right.** A coal stove in 1937.

 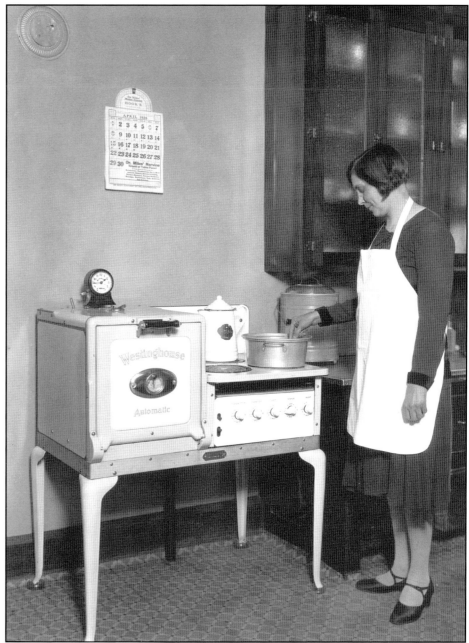

Left. A workhorse of a coal stove. Note the irons on top of the warmer. **Right.** An electric range in 1928.

Above. Lots of little details to notice in this photo from 1932 of Mrs. Jack Ralston and son in her orderly and functional kitchen. The sink faucet has three knobs: one for cold, one for hot and one for mixed.

In the Kitchen   **37**

Above. Taking the time to provide useful, loving instruction in the art of canning jar washing.

Above. Canning mustard greens for winter use. Note that in both of the photos on this page, the sinks have three water sources. The sink in the photo above has two faucets and a pump. The sink to the left has three faucets. One faucet might be providing "soft" rainwater captured in a cistern or other reservoir.

38 America's Rural Yesterday

Above. This Sellers kitchen cabinet included many useful features, including a weights and measures chart and a list of "Shortcuts and Helpful Hints for the Kitchen" inside the flour sifter cabinet door.

In the Kitchen 39

Above. Twin daughters of Mrs Clark Baker watch as she spoons mashed potatoes into a serving dish.

Above. A frosted layer cake and pie await on the sideboard as the young man washes up before dinner. A combination gas range and electric stove and new Kelvinator refrigeration unit provide modern conveniences in this 1930 home.

In the Kitchen   41

Above. Mrs. Fred Orth of Terre Haute, Indiana, with her Kelvinator electric refrigerator.

Above. An electric refrigerator in the farm kitchen of Mrs. Herman Klusmeier of Terre Haute, Indiana.

42 America's Rural Yesterday

Right. An impressive pressure cooker sits atop the cookstove as a farm wife cans vegetables.

Opposite. Maxine Gardner and Betty Carmony can foods in Manilla, Indiana, as part of their 4-H Club work.

In the Kitchen 43

44 America's Rural Yesterday

Above. This photo provided counterpoint to the photo near right.
Near Right. The notation on the back of this photograph reads "An electric washer takes much of the drudgery out of laundry work."
Opposite. Mrs. A. L. Goodwin, Wanatah, Indiana, washing in her farm kitchen. 1926.

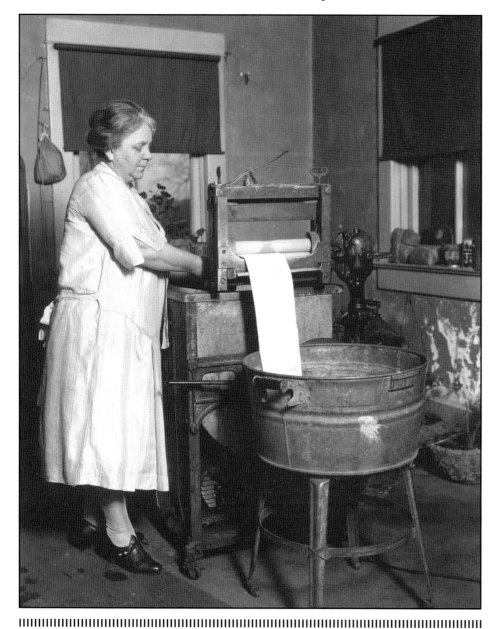

Above. Mrs. Daniel Bechtal of Goshen, Indiana, and her electrically-operated washing machine. 1928.

Above. Laundering by hand with a washboard.

Housework 47

Left. An electric washing machine, large utility sink and room for hanging laundry makes the work easier.

Above. A wagon wheel raises and lowers the clothes line, which appears to be anchored to a cultipacker.

Above. With a pocketful of clothespins, the farm wife hangs the laundry on wash day.

Above. Martha Allen of West Lafayette, Indiana, uses an electric iron.

Housework 51

Above. A wall-mounted ironing board.

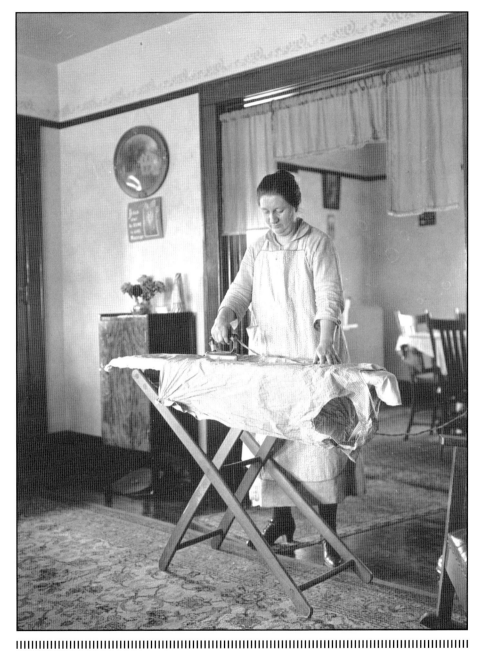

Above. Mrs. Mervin Eby, of Elkhart, Indiana, with an electric iron.

52 America's Rural Yesterday

Above. Mrs. Chalmer Miller of Moran, Indiana, sews clothes for her four daughters.
Upper Right. Mrs. Grover Arbogast of Selma, Indiana, uses her electric sewing machine.
Lower Right. A Singer machine with built-in light.

Housework 53

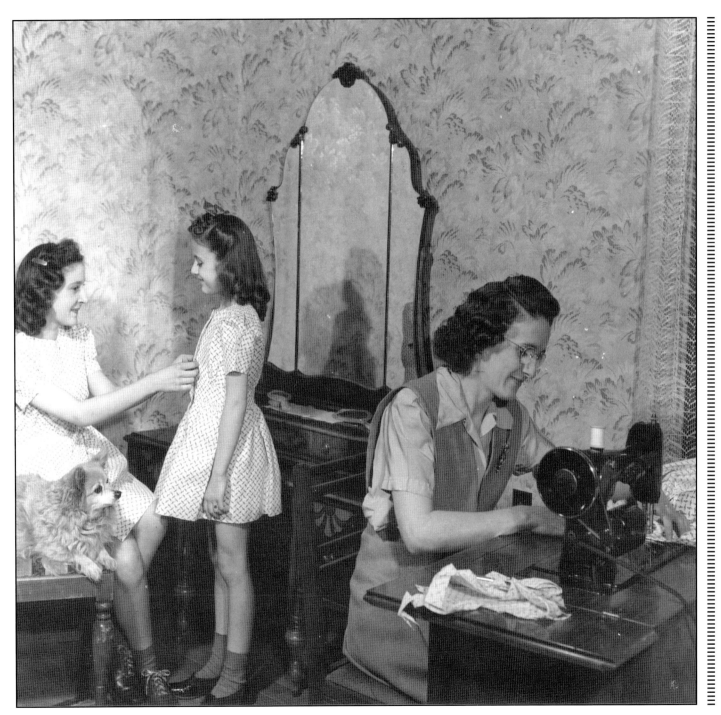

Left. Sewing matching dresses in 1945.

54   America's Rural Yesterday

Housework

Opposite. Electric vacuum cleaners made keeping floors and carpets clean much easier.
Above. Twin girls watch as their mother uses an electric vacuum cleaner in 1930. Notice the side table pushed up against the fireplace during the summer months.

56 America's Rural Yesterday

Right. The team obscures the vehicle or implement behind them but it is fair to say the way was fairly tough going.

Opposite. Muddy conditions led to rutted roads in rural Iowa in 1919.

Chapter 5
Going to Town

58 America's Rural Yesterday

Going to Town   **59**

Opposite. Southern Indiana in 1933 .

Above. Similar model of car as in opposite photo but this time stuck in the snow.

60 America's Rural Yesterday

Right. A Case tractor pulls a truck loaded with rice out of a ditch on the farm of Henry Bull, Stuggart, Arkansas.

Opposite. A ferry transports a truck loaded with grain across the Arkansas River near Gillett, Arkansas.

Going to Town 61

Above Left. Hauling a load to town from the John Morris farm, New Richmond, Indiana.
Above Right. Dropping off the mail on the way to Lafayette, Indiana, from the R.A. Foresman farm.
Opposite. A family of four goes to town on their farm wagon pulled by a lovely and fit team of Belgians.

64 America's Rural Yesterday

Right. A farm boy delivers cream to the market on a bicycle in 1914.

Going to Town **65**

Above Left. A family picks up eggs and other farm goods to take home.

Left. A goat cart travels over a brick-paved street in town.

Above. Kermit Sands and Floyd Houser, near Center Point, Indiana, driving their pony to a cart.

Going to Town 67

Above. A pony takes a mother and five children for a ride in 1915.

68 America's Rural Yesterday

Above. Grading the gravel of an Indiana State Highway in 1932.
Opposite. Covered bridges protected the roadway from weather. This one stood in Shelbyville, Indiana.

Going to Town 69

Going to Town 71

Opposite. A roadside market on the farm of Henry Tennessen of Oshkosh, Wisconsin.
Above. Home made ice cream being churned for sale at roadside market in Texas.

72   America's Rural Yesterday

Above. A family crosses an Indiana street in 1936.

Opposite. A lunch counter in 1953.

74 America's Rural Yesterday

Above and Right. Before the development of computers and internet access, books and the libraries that loaned them were where people sought knowledge.

Opposite. Mobile libraries made scheduled stops in rural areas inside trailers.

In Town 77

Opposite. Mail delivery with a handsome and alert horse.

Top Left. These boys display their means of production and distribution for the camera. 1920.

Bottom Left. The Kleen Milk Dairy advertised that its milk came from "tuberculin tested herds."

Opposite. An iceman makes a delivery in 1937.

Top Left. A coal delivery in 1935.

Bottom Left. A gasoline tank truck fills the tanks at a Shell station in 1937.

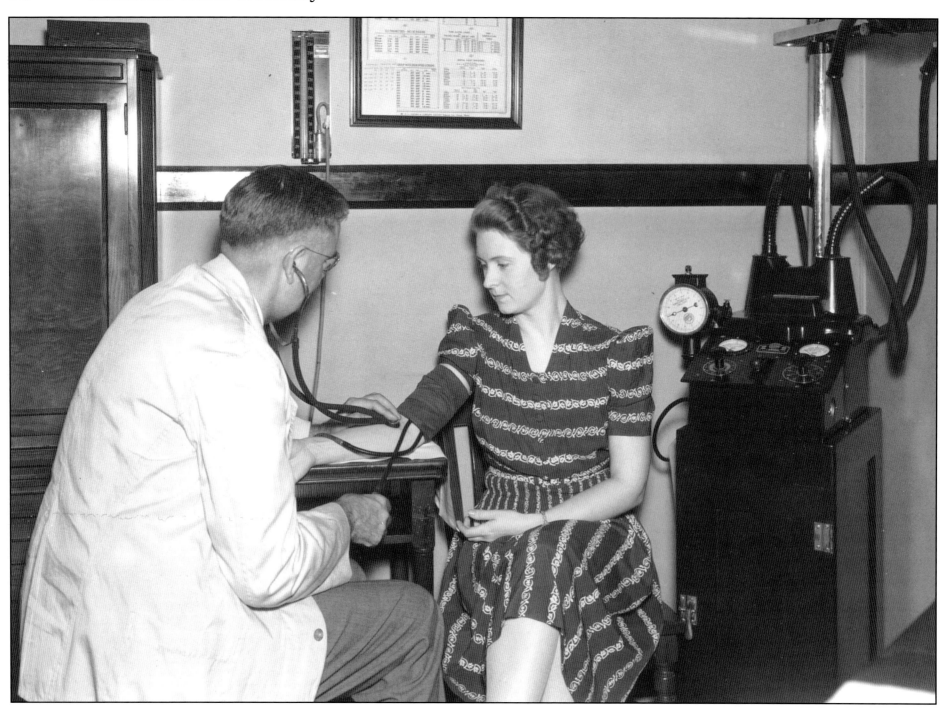

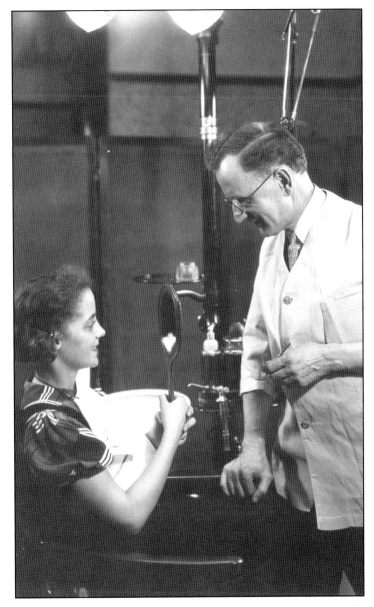

Opposite. Taking a blood pressure reading.
Above Left. Preserving a pretty smile.
Above Right. Operating the telephone switchboard.

82 America's Rural Yesterday

Above. This clearly staged photo has a caption on the back: "Boys caught playing with fire. Fires are easier to start than to stop."

In Town 83

Above Left. A few moments later, the firemen staged a "rescuing a cat from a tree" photo.
Above Right. The Lafayette, Indiana, policeman has his pen out to write a ticket in 1941.

Above. A small country store in Indiana.

In Town 85

Left. The general store offered news, gossip, a warm stove, and a game of checkers. 1938.

In Town 87

Opposite. A sewing class in Crawfordsville, Indiana, in 1922.

Top Left. Sewing Club.

Bottom Left. A group of young men attend what appears to be a 4-H youth leader meeting.

Top Right. Small town in western Indiana in 1938.

Bottom Right. Greencastle, Indiana, 1931.

Opposite. A busy small town.

In Town **91**

Opposite. Ice cream sodas provide a treat.

Left. Two scoops for fifty cents.

Right. Buying vegetable seed in spring.

Opposite. A well-stocked and organized dry goods store.

Above. A crowded general store.
Opposite. Ritter's Feeds, Seeds and Supplies served the local farming community.

America's Rural Yesterday

Shopping 97

Opposite. Stores in the 1930s. **Above.** A traveling grocery delivers flour to a customer in 1935.

Shopping 99

Left. The local poultry feed salesman buys chickens when he drops off feed.
Left. Fresh milk delivered right to your door.

Above. The General Store in Twelve Mile, Indiana, also housed the local branch library.

Above. A pharmacy in 1944.

Above. A farmer tests the handles on a new garden cultivator at his local hardware store.

Above. A salesman explains the features of the latest tractors and attachments.

104 America's Rural Yesterday

Shopping **105**

Opposite. A Buick automobile dealer also sold and serviced Allis Chalmers tractors in Walkerton, Indiana, in 1937.
Above. Filling stations were all full service in 1932 when this photo was taken.

Opposite and Above. A fourth grade class in 1935. Lots of little details here, including all the fresh cut flowers along the windows.

108　America's Rural Yesterday

Left. The same fourth grade class pictured on the preceeding pages.

Above and Opposite. When school was out, young people might study in the "juvenile" section at the local library. West Lafayette, Indiana.

At School 109

110 America's Rural Yesterday

Above. "Milk Time" during a school trip. 1920.

Opposite. Seventh grade English class.

At School 111

Above. Boys were taught industrial arts such as in this middle school woodworking class.

Above. Girls were taught home economics such as in this high school sewing class.

114   America's Rural Yesterday

At School   115

Opposite and Above. Off to school.

116   America's Rural Yesterday

Top Right. A Wakarusa, Indiana, school bus in 1930.

Bottom Right. A Tippecanoe County, Indiana, school bus in 1935.

Opposite. School buses loading at Sheffield Township (Indiana) High School in 1935.

At School

Top Right. Three crossing guards and a policeman stop traffic as students cross the streets.

Bottom Right. A policeman helps grade school children cross at the corner.

Opposite. Playground outside the Mitchell, Indiana, consolidated school, featuring a very tall set of slides.

At School 119

120 America's Rural Yesterday

Above. A game of some sort that resembles team tag.

122   America's Rural Yesterday

Right. High school girls playing baseball.

Opposite. A game of barefoot baseball in 1933.

Chapter 9
Leisure Time

124 America's Rural Yesterday

Above and Opposite. A game of croquet was a common pastime in town and in the country.

Leisure Time   **125**

Right and Opposite. A game of horseshoes was taken very seriously by participants and spectators.

Leisure Time **127**

Leisure Time **129**

Opposite. Donald and Frances Bowman play tennis at their farm home near Rockfield, Indiana.
Above. Playing tennis on the farm of I.J. Mathews of Winamac, Indiana.

Leisure Time **131**

Opposite. Middle school boys play a game of backyard football.

Left. High School basketball players pose for the photographer.

Right. Fishing and camping trip on the Flambeau River in northern Wisconsin. 1923.

Opposite. Camping in 1924.

Leisure Time **135**

Opposite. An outdoor evening cookout.

Left. A hot picnic lunch in 1921.

136   America's Rural Yesterday

Leisure Time **137**

Opposite and Left. Camping and fishing in 1923.

138   America's Rural Yesterday

Opposite and Left. Strapping on skates and taking to the ice.

Leisure Time 139

140 America's Rural Yesterday

Leisure Time **141**

Opposite. Family time on the farm with a great Percheron farm horse that is patient, loyal and willing. 1933.
Above. Another terrific scene with a pony pulling two sleds.

Above and Opposite. Pulling the sled to the sledding hill.

144 America's Rural Yesterday

Right. Building a snowman.

Opposite. One boy pulls another on a sled near Buck Creek, Indiana.

Leisure Time 145

Above. Trying their luck at the creek.

Leisure Time **147**

Above. Fishing in Lake Decatur near Decatur, Illinois.

Above. A homemade swimming hole on a hot farm day. **Opposite.** Swimming with friends.

Leisure Time 149

Above. Boy Scouts in 1937.

Leisure Time 151

Above. Boys on a camping trip.

152   America's Rural Yesterday

Above. 4-H boys and girls learning folk dancing.   **Opposite.** An outdoor dance at Purdue University.

Leisure Time 153

Above. A shot of the crowd on the midway at the 1928 Indiana State Fair.

Leisure Time 155

Above. Game of chance at a county fair.

Above. Parade advertising the Indiana State Fair dog show in 1930.